P9-DCR-419

P9-DCR-419

Essential Question
Where can you find patterns in nature?

Weather Patterns

by James McNaughton

Introduction

When you have an exciting outdoor event such as a picnic coming up, chances are that you check the weather forecast. These days you can be pretty sure that it will be correct.

Weather is complicated, and it used to be really hard to predict. However, prediction has gotten much better because scientists understand much more about how weather works.

The sun's heat drives our weather. Warm air rises and moves away from hot places, such as the **tropics**, to cooler places. The hot air pushes down the heavier, cooler air, which moves into the space that the warm air has left. The result of hot and cold air moving is wind. This wind usually moves in regular patterns.

Meteorologists, scientists who study weather, look for patterns in the weather. They do this to make weather predictions even more accurate. Meteorologists are able to predict the things that make up everyday weather such as clouds, wind, and **precipitation**. They can also predict events, such as hurricanes and tornadoes.

However, some weather is just weird. It doesn't follow the normal rules or keep to a regular pattern. There is still a lot to learn before we will be able to predict the weather with complete accuracy.

Hurricanes occur annually in tropical and subtropical parts of the world.

Weather is driven by the distribution of the sun's heat in our **atmosphere**. Some places are hotter and some are colder. When air heats up, it gets less dense, so it expands and rises. Then it moves to where the cold air is. The cold air is forced down. This movement of hot and cold air creates wind.

The sun's rays are stronger, or hotter, at the **equator**. They get weaker, or colder, toward the North and South poles since they receive less direct sunlight. Land masses create areas of warmer air. Land absorbs the sun's heat and releases it into the atmosphere faster than oceans. The wind caused by hot and cold air moving around occurs in regular patterns that meteorologists can predict.

Intense Tropical Heat

The tropics are hot since they get the most direct sunlight. Hot air moves away from the tropics and makes wind.

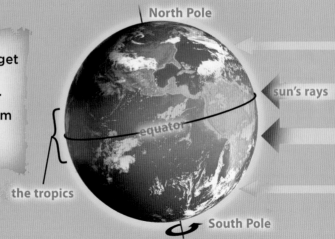

North Pole

sun's rays

equator

the tropics

South Pole

The sun's heat also moves around through a process called the water cycle. When the sun heats water, some of it **evaporates** and becomes water vapor. The water vapor, which is not usually visible, rises and cools down in the atmosphere. Then the water vapor **condenses**, causing the formation of clouds. Eventually some of this moisture falls as precipitation, such as rain, and the cycle begins again.

The repetition of this cycle redistributes a lot of the sun's heat. The water cycle also produces regular local weather patterns, such as cloud formations over mountains.

The Water Cycle

Most of the moisture in our atmosphere comes from the ocean, although some also evaporates from rivers and lakes. A small amount of moisture comes from plants.

Water condenses to form clouds.

Water evaporates.

Water precipitates.

Water flows into rivers or soaks into the ground, then returns to oceans.

Prevailing Wind

Wherever you live in the world, there is a prevailing wind. A prevailing wind is the regular wind in your area. Much of the weather in the United States comes from the west because of a prevailing westerly wind. You might not appreciate this wind if you have to ride your bike into it!

When warm air spreads north and south away from the tropics, Earth's rotation makes the wind curve. This is known as the Coriolis effect. As a result of the Coriolis effect, the **temperate zones** in both **hemispheres** have prevailing westerlies, or winds that come from the west.

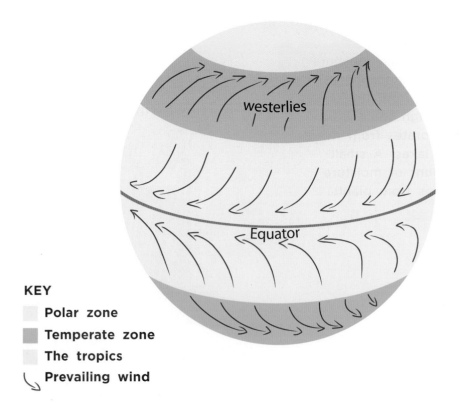

KEY
- Polar zone
- Temperate zone
- The tropics
- Prevailing wind

Prevailing winds can also come from local conditions. Sea breezes, for example, are a regular weather pattern. They occur on hot, sunny days when the land heats up much faster than the water. This causes the air above the land to get warm, rise, and spread offshore over the ocean. Cooler air over the ocean moves in to replace the warm air, blowing over the land as a cooling sea breeze.

In Fremantle, Australia, it's very hot. Locals call the summer sea breeze the Fremantle Doctor because contact with the cool air is such a relief!

Sea breezes often begin to blow in the afternoon. Land breezes are caused when the land cools off faster than the water. These usually begin at night.

Chapter 2
Seasonal Weather

Many weather events happen at the same time each year. Seasons follow a predictable pattern. If you live in a temperate zone, you have four seasons. If you live in the tropics, there are only two seasons: wet and dry. Monsoon and hurricane seasons occur when seasonal temperatures, combined with other circumstances, create the right conditions for them.

Monsoons

These intense seasonal rains happen when the prevailing wind reverses, or changes direction. In India and Southeast Asia, this occurs when super-heated air over the land rises, pulling in wet air from the sea. This causes rain. Lots of rain!

The Southeast Asian Monsoon

The monsoon season usually happens between June and September every year. For many places, this season provides the only significant rain all year. This rain is extremely important to the agriculture and economy of the region. **Torrential** rains and flooding are also common during the monsoon season.

The North American Monsoon

The North American monsoon season usually begins in the middle of summer. Moist, warm air begins to move inland over central Mexico from the Gulf of Mexico and the Gulf of California. Heavy rain falls in the mountains of central Mexico. The monsoon then moves north, bringing rain to Arizona, New Mexico, and Texas in the United States.

This rain is the main source of water for the desert in this area, so it's very important to life. Firefighters also appreciate its help. This area of the Southwest is so dry that wildfires are very common.

How the North American Monsoon Works

Just like the Southeast Asian monsoon, rising hot air draws in cooler, moister ocean air to cause the North American monsoon.

moist air   moist air

hot air   hot air   hot air

Hurricanes and Tornadoes

There are other types of regular weather patterns that aren't as helpful as monsoons. Hurricanes and tornadoes can cause huge damage to man-made structures and even loss of life. Luckily, however, these strong storms can be predicted to some degree. They have regular seasons and typical locations.

The Atlantic hurricane season begins in June and lasts through to the end of November. During this time, hot rising air and warm ocean water combine to make hurricane conditions.

Hurricanes, typhoons, and tropical cyclones are the same thing—they just have different names in different parts of the world.

Tornadoes occur over land instead of over water, but like hurricanes, they form in warm, wet air. Some states experience many more tornadoes than others. These states are in an area known as Tornado Alley. Tornadoes hit Tornado Alley from late spring through early summer.

Tornadoes form when dry air from Canada and the Rocky Mountains meets warm, moist air from the Gulf of Mexico and hot, dry air from the Sonoran Desert. These three wind patterns combine to form thunderstorms and an unstable atmosphere. These conditions can also create tornadoes.

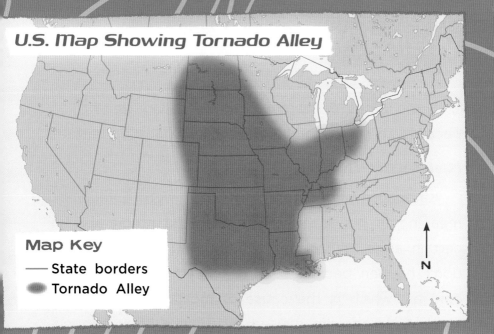

U.S. Map Showing Tornado Alley

Map Key
— State borders
● Tornado Alley

N ↑

Hurricanes Versus Tornadoes

Hurricanes

Hurricanes are severe tropical storms that form over warm water. Hurricane winds can exceed 150 miles per hour. They blow in a large spiral around a mostly calm center known as the "eye." The size of the storm can range from 25 to 600 miles (40 to 965 kilometers) in diameter. Hurricanes can last from several days to more than two weeks.

Tornadoes

A tornado is a violent windstorm characterized by a twisting, funnel-shaped cloud. It usually grows out of a thunderstorm. Winds in a tornado can blow as fast as 320 miles per hour. In the middle is an eye of air spinning downward. The eye is surrounded by a strong upward current, or pull. Tornadoes are much smaller than hurricanes, but they are still powerful enough to lift houses into the air and rip trees out of the ground. They usually last less than ten minutes.

Some types of weather can be called weird because they don't follow the usual rules or patterns.

Katabatic Winds

Katabatic winds (from the Greek word *katabaino*, meaning to go down) are regular and predictable in certain areas. What makes them weird is that they don't happen because of the movement of hot and cold air, which is the cause of most winds. Instead, katabatic winds are caused by gravity. They happen when cold air "falls" down a slope. They are most common in the **polar zones**, especially in Greenland and Antarctica. Here cold air builds up on high, frozen plateaus, and then "slides" downhill to the ocean.

When cold air makes contact with snow and ice, it becomes even denser. Katabatic winds can reach speeds of up to 150 miles per hour. They can even erode stone.

Katabatic winds are unusual and only occur in a few places on Earth.

A katabatic wind with a very different effect is the Santa Ana wind in California. The Santa Ana wind occurs when cool air from the Great Basin, the high desert between the Rocky Mountains and the Sierra Nevada range, falls downhill over the Sierra Nevada. The wind heats up and gets even hotter on its way to the southern California coast. The Santa Ana wind blows during the dry season. It can be dangerous because it makes wildfires spread quickly.

Sierra Nevada

Great Basin

California

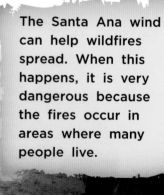

The Santa Ana wind can help wildfires spread. When this happens, it is very dangerous because the fires occur in areas where many people live.

El Niño

Another example of weird weather is El Niño *(el NEE-nyo)*. El Niño is a large and complicated weather event. Sometimes it occurs every second year. Other times it can be seven years between each El Niño. So far scientists have been unable to predict it. During an El Niño cycle, the water in the Pacific Ocean along the northern coast of South America warms up. This changes normal ocean currents. The warm ocean water also changes normal weather patterns.

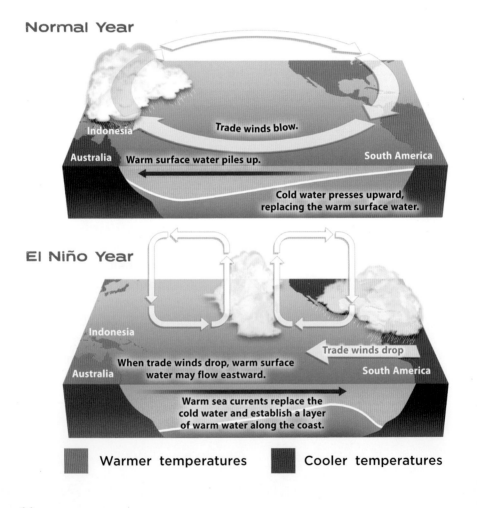

Normal Year

Indonesia

Australia

Trade winds blow.

Warm surface water piles up.

South America

Cold water presses upward, replacing the warm surface water.

El Niño Year

Indonesia

Australia

Trade winds drop

When trade winds drop, warm surface water may flow eastward.

South America

Warm sea currents replace the cold water and establish a layer of warm water along the coast.

Warmer temperatures   Cooler temperatures

El Niño can cause prevailing weather patterns to reverse. Dry parts of South America can flood. Wet areas across the Pacific in places such as Indonesia and Australia, can experience drought. Areas such as California and Washington may experience very cold winters as a result of El Niño.

How much impact an El Niño event has depends on how much ocean temperatures increase. A small rise of about 4 or 5 degrees Fahrenheit will result in only a minor effect. A big increase in the ocean's temperature (14 to 18 degrees Fahrenheit) causes major changes in weather around the globe.

A small rise in water temperature in the eastern Pacific Ocean can have far-reaching consequences, such as a long, terrible drought in Australia.

Conclusion

Studying patterns in the weather allows us to better understand and predict what weather will do. Some people long ago thought that wind was the breath of the gods, but now we know that wind is caused by the effect of the sun's heat in the atmosphere. We know that wind blows in predictable ways, and we understand why there are prevailing winds. We also understand the way the water cycle redistributes heat.

Weird weather is harder to understand because it doesn't have predictable patterns. Katabatic winds are the result of cold air being pulled downhill by gravity.

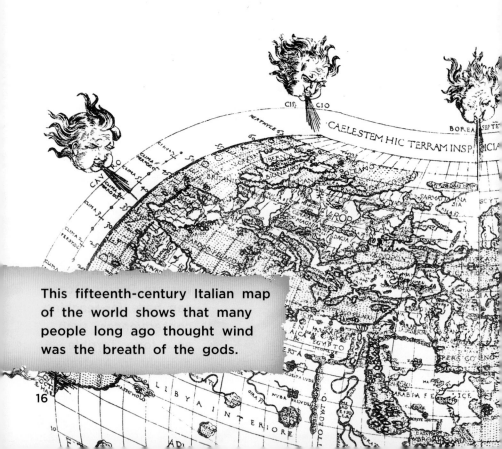

This fifteenth-century Italian map of the world shows that many people long ago thought wind was the breath of the gods.

El Niño is so big and complicated that we don't fully understand it, but we do know that a relatively small change in the temperature of the Pacific Ocean in one place can have a big effect on weather far away.

Today weather satellites give us a much clearer picture of what's happening. Meteorologists around the world work together to figure out global weather patterns. Even though meteorologists are much better at predicting the weather now, they can still get it wrong sometimes. We've come a long way, but there is always more to learn.

Weather satellites take pictures from high above Earth so we can see what's happening with the world's weather.

Respond to Reading

Summarize

Use key details from the text to summarize what you have learned about weather patterns. Your graphic organizer may help you.

Main Idea
Detail
Detail
Detail

Text Evidence

1. What evidence can you use to show that *Weather Patterns* is expository text? GENRE

2. What is the main idea of the first paragraph on page 9? Give key details to support your answer. MAIN IDEA AND KEY DETAILS

3. The word *cyclones* on page 10 contains the Greek root *cycl*, which means "circle or ring." Using this information and context clues, what do you think the word *cyclone* means? GREEK ROOTS

4. The main idea of the first paragraph on page 15 is that *El Niño changes normal weather patterns.* Write about why this is the main idea. WRITE ABOUT READING

Compare Texts
Read about how people have used cloud patterns to predict the weather.

CLOUD ATLAS

People have used clouds to predict weather for thousands of years. However, the nature of clouds and what causes them remained a mystery for a long time.

In 1803, an Englishman named Luke Howard suggested that there was a fixed number of cloud types. Other people had thought there were thousands because clouds always look so different. Howard saw a pattern that no one else had seen. He said there were just a few families of clouds. He gave them names such as *cirrus* (Latin for hair), *cumulus* (Latin for heap), and *stratus* (Latin for layer). This new idea changed meteorology forever.

cirrus

cumulus

stratus

Howard's system also grouped clouds into three height categories. Cirrus describes both a type of cloud and a height (the highest). Stratus is a type of cloud and also the lowest cloud level. *Alto* clouds are in the middle.

The system included other names, too. For example, a *nimbus* cloud is a rain cloud. By combining a few Latin names, you can describe lots of different clouds.

Clouds are very helpful in weather forecasting. For example, significant precipitation usually comes from *nimbostratus* and *cumulonimbus* clouds. Cumulus clouds can cause showers, and stratus clouds can cause drizzle. Cirrus clouds are made of ice particles.

Cumulonimbus clouds are unique in that they can rise through all three cloud levels.

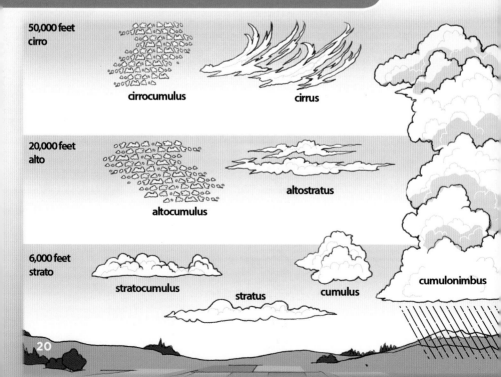

50,000 feet
cirro

cirrocumulus

cirrus

20,000 feet
alto

altocumulus

altostratus

6,000 feet
strato

stratocumulus

stratus

cumulus

cumulonimbus

Before the telegraph was invented, cloud patterns could be used only to predict local weather. The telegraph allowed descriptions of clouds and the weather predicted by them to be sent quickly to people outside a local area.

If people had all described the clouds in their own way, it would have been confusing. However, everyone used a standard cloud atlas based on Howard's system. This meant cloud types could be clearly labeled. People far away knew exactly what kinds of clouds were being described, so meteorology became a more exact science.

Luke Howard was a chemist with an interest in weather. His use of names in Latin, the language of science, helped his cloud classification system make a worldwide impact.

Make Connections

How did the invention of the telegraph help people predict weather? ESSENTIAL QUESTION

What are some of the ways people have used patterns in clouds and the pattern of the seasons to understand weather? TEXT TO TEXT

Glossary

atmosphere *(AT-muh-sfeer)* the layer of gases surrounding a planet *(page 4)*

condenses *(kahn-DEN-sez)* when a gas becomes a liquid; for example, water vapor becomes liquid water *(page 5)*

equator *(i-KWAY-tuhr)* the imaginary line drawn halfway between the poles, which divides Earth into a northern and a southern hemisphere *(page 4)*

evaporates *(i-VAP-uh-rayts)* when a liquid becomes a gas; for example, liquid water becomes water vapor *(page 5)*

hemispheres *(HEM-i-sfirz)* the northern and southern halves of Earth, as divided by the equator *(page 6)*

polar zones *(POH-luhr zohnz)* the two zones on Earth where the climate is extremely cold, located at the North and South poles *(page 12)*

precipitation *(pri-si-puh-TAY-shuhn)* general name for water in any form falling from clouds; for example, rain, snow, and hail *(page 2)*

temperate zones *(TEM-puh-ruht zohnz)* the two zones on Earth where the climate isn't too hot or too cold, located approximately midway between the tropics and the poles *(page 6)*

torrential *(taw-REN-shuhl)* quickly falling in large amounts *(page 8)*

tropics *(TRAH-piks)* the zone around Earth's equator that is closest to the sun and where the climate is typically hot *(page 2)*

Index

Focus on Science

Purpose To show how warmed air affects the weather

Procedure

Step 1 ➤ Cut a circle out of paper, then cut the circle to form a spiral.

Step 2 ➤ Tie a piece of string or yarn to one end of the spiral.

Step 3 ➤ Have your teacher turn on a heat source, such as a lamp. Carefully hold or hang the spiral about 12 inches above the heat source.

Step 4 ➤ Describe what the spiral does. Turn off the heat source, but continue to hold your spiral above it. Observe what happens.

Conclusion Just as the sun produces heat, the heat source also produced heat. When air heats up, either from the sun or from another heat source, something happens. What happened when you held the spiral above the heat source? What happened when you turned the heat source off? How do you think this activity relates to what you learned about weather?